15 Steps to Finding

A Woman's Journey

Melissa Davis

Acknowledgments:

To the women who shared their stories,

You are courageous and brave. It was a pleasure to hear you speak and listen to your truths, as your stories set the atmosphere for every lesson in this book. I thank you for being vulnerable. You all possess a strength that many seek: a self-awareness that is both unapologetic and undeniable.

To my final editor,

Safira, you are amazing! You got me through the last leg of this race and helped me to the finish line. Thank you for preserving the voices and tone of the book while slaying the edits and keeping me on track.

To my children,

Never stop dreaming. Never stop making those dreams a reality. And no matter what, never give up. Mommy and Daddy love you.

To my family and friends,

Thank you for your support and words of encouragement. Without you all, I don't think I would have made it. Jayne, Marilyn, Steven and Amy, you are my family. From being my college professors to becoming life-long friends, one of my dreams is to make you all proud.

To everyone else who helped me along the way, thank you.

To my readers,

Thank you for picking up this book, I created it for you. I want you to be a better version of who you were yesterday, so keep trying, my love. You will fall sometimes and that's okay. This book is here to help you get back up.

Disclaimer:

Some names have been changed to protect the identities of the women who wished to remain anonymous.

Table of Contents

"What if…
everything you're going through
is preparing you…
for what you asked for?"
--Unknown

Step 1: Discover Who You Are

What do you know about yourself? Simply put, self-identity is simply understanding what makes you, YOU. Some women have a strong sense of who they are, and it shows. It shows through how they embrace their sexuality, how they dress, how they speak, who they date, and who they love. By that same token, having little sense of your identity also shows. That's why it's important to learn about who you are.

This book is all about learning who you are so you can find the right person for you. Don't be scared. The journey that you will experience in this book will make you stronger, more empowered, and ready to find love.

Sarah:

I was the seventh of eleven children born to two sharecroppers. The church was top priority outside of work'n. We would go to St. Peter's Disciple Church early in the morn'n and leave late at night every Sunday, and there would be school and prayer meetings at home during the week. I never really thought much about college. Back in those days, get'n an education higher than primary school was slim. We were too poor to do anything but work and segregation was so bad we knew work'n wouldn't make us rich, but get us to the next day. See, we lived in Kingston, North Carolina, before the Civil Rights Movement. Understand'n who you were and what you wanted to be was a luxury we just couldn't afford.

Salina:

I'm only 29, but I know I'm a nurturer. I take care of people. When my grandma got sick, it was all about taking care of her. I bring this type of care into all my relationships. Growing up, I didn't have many friends and wasn't really social, but the friends I did have were like my family and I made sure they felt it. I take care of my two daughters the most. Meeting people's needs is how I show them that I love them.

Xuan:

Can you imagine growing up in a Vietnamese American household and living in a blue-collar town like Harrisburg, Virginia? I grew up with three older brothers and a little sister. My sister and I weren't allowed the same freedom as my brothers because we were—well, girls. Born in Vietnam during the fall of Saigon, we moved to New Jersey when I was one. I grew up in a very traditional, male privileged household. My brothers got to stay out late, didn't have to babysit, and got to date. But because I was a young girl, I was expected to stay home and watch my baby sister. So, when I got older it was hard to know what or who I was.

Tesia:

I was enjoying my 27-year-old life. I was in the army, on my way home from Fort Hood, where I was stationed when I got the call. I had a girlfriend for a while and was just living my best life. I didn't know anything about my old schoolmate's baby when she called me to pick her up. I went to the floor of the hospital where she was. At that very moment, she was signing the papers to hand her child over to the state. I saw this tiny little brown skinned baby wrapped up in a blanket going into a system that wouldn't take care of her. It was at that moment I knew I had to do something.

Jene:

As a child growing up in the early 70s, I would sneak to my Uncle's candy store; it wasn't far from my grandmother's house. We lived in a close-knit South Philadelphia neighborhood where Black businesses were beginning to resurface. My mother had eleven children so you could imagine the chaos we caused, but my uncle didn't seem to mind. Every time we got candy, I remember thinking that I wanted to have my own business like him. I remember going to the store every day, seeing him at the counter, and we were so proud to say he was our uncle because in the black neighborhood during those times, generating income in your own community made you a local celebrity. I wanted that, whatever it was.

Star:

My siblings and I were born to two crackheads, and we were all in foster care. My parents would visit the foster home I was in every once-in-a-while. I remember seeing my mom a few times around my fifth birthday.

Welcome! So far, you have been introduced to six of the eleven women who will be with you throughout this book. Their stories are meant to help you until you have completed the book or found love. After each round of stories, there will be activities for you to complete. Don't be alarmed. I don't want you to protest in the streets, nude— just yet! The activities will be preparations for your real-life tests. And believe me, there will be many. The idea is to make sure that these voices are what you hear when you need them most.

Can you hear it?

Just listen.

Remember Salina, the 29-year-old amazing mother of two girls? Like Salina, many women who have been introduced to caretaker roles early in life realize many years later that they never thought about their own needs and wants. They never had time to consider putting themselves first and had never done so. Now, this is not all bad. In fact, selflessness is a rare, yet beautiful quality to possess. However, it can lead to a life of insecurity. This caretaker quality can create a feeling of being unappreciated and make you dependent on the well-being of others for your happiness. If you are realizing for the first time that perhaps caring for others has stopped you from caring for yourself, this exercise may be a bit challenging. But don't worry. We're gonna get through this together.

Step 1 - Activity

Part 1: Today is Month_____ Day_____
Year_____

What is your name? What does it mean?

_____

_____

_____

_____

Who gave you your name? Is there a story behind it? If so, what?

_____

_____

_____

_____

_____

_____

How would you describe yourself?

_____

_____

_____

_____

_____

_____

_____

_____

_____

_____

What made you choose those words to describe yourself?

_____

_____

_____

_____

_____

When you look in the mirror, what do you see?

_____

_____

_____

_____

_____

What are some of your childhood memories?

_____

_____

_____

_____

_____

_____

_____

_____

_____

_____

_____

_____

How does your childhood shape who you are?

_____

_____

_____

_____

_____

_____

_____

_____

_____

_____

_____

_____

_____

_____

_____

_____

Part 2

Now that you have answered these questions, reflect on what you've written.

Don't forget that the objective of this exercise is to discover or re-discover who you are. Find out what makes you, YOU! Ask yourself these questions every so often, and if the answers change, Great. Change is good.

Part 3

What are your political, spiritual, and religious beliefs?

_____
_____
_____
_____
_____
_____
_____
_____
_____

Do you have fears? What are they? If not, why don't you?

_____
_____
_____
_____
_____
_____
_____

What are you looking for out of life?

_____
_____
_____
_____
_____
_____
_____

What are some things you think about when you are alone?

_____

_____

_____

_____

_____

_____

What are some things you struggle with?

_____

_____

_____

_____

_____

_____

What are some things about yourself you'd like to work on?

_____

_____

_____

_____

_____

You don't have to answer the questions all at once, and you don't have to answer them alone. You can work on them by yourself or during a session with your therapist. Take your time through these steps as they will help build your foundation.

Step 2: Choose the Therapy for You

Focusing this step on one person was a difficult choice, as many of the women in this book all great examples of how important therapy is to personal growth. I want you pay close attention to Nichole's experience. I understand the stigma of going to therapy, as it can feel different or uncomfortable when you first reflect on your thoughts and feelings. I'm here to tell you not to worry. Although your therapy may be different from Nichole's, being able to dissect and reflect on your thoughts and feelings is taking your first giant step toward healing.

Nicole:

My insurance only paid for a community health therapist, but I was still grateful. I only worked seasonal jobs at the time and couldn't afford the resource on my own.

Her name was Tiffany, and she was one of three Bi-racial siblings. In the beginning, I would see her once a week. The sessions were sometimes quiet because I had nothing to say. My thoughts were afraid to come out to someone I didn't know.

I had been to therapy before as a child and again in college, but it didn't really help. Besides, therapy was supposed to be for white people, or so I thought. I told Tiffany that and she just laughed and said, "That's what I thought too before going to school to be a Therapist". As the weeks passed, I started to feel more comfortable, talking to her like she was one of the friends I could never keep. First, she'd listen. Looking back, I think that was what helped me the most. We were both in our late 20's and she always had a way of relating to my feelings and giving me uninterrupted venting time. At times, she would give me a different perspective and exercises to help channel my thoughts in a more positive direction. Going to therapy was more like having a friend rather than a 'therapist'.

Step 2 - Activity

Part 1:

Before you get help, it's best to determine the type of help that will support your journey. I know you're thinking, "Well, I don't know what types would help me," but don't worry. First, analyze what you're struggling with. You formed your identity in Step 1, now use your discoveries to write down what you need help with.

_____

_____

_____

_____

_____

_____

_____

_____

_____

_____

_____

_____

_____

_____

_____

_____

Once you realize you need a little help, you can choose the best therapy for your needs.

Here are some therapies that helped me in my journey, and may help you:

- **Create or buy a book** to use as a journal (I have created this very book with that in mind). Be sure to write in your journal often and revisit what you've written every few months, so you can add updates and responses. It may seem strange now, but you will thank me later.

- **Talk to an elder.** Befriend a grandparent, older neighbor in the community, or teacher that you can trust. You will be surprised how understanding elders can be since they have dealt with many of the things you are going through.

- **Spend more time with younger people,** like children, if you are able to. Young people are carefree and can be great for just appreciating the small pleasures in life. They are blunt and curious and full of energy. This can help with getting to the root of your unhappiness and discovering that you can still be cherished unconditionally.

Don't be afraid to explore other ways to be stronger, wiser, and more loving of self. You are your best weapon against all those negative thoughts that get in the way of healing.

Part 2:

Write down other options for approaching your healing journey.

_____

_____

_____

_____

_____

Step 3: Understand Your Self-Worth

You are doing GREAT!

You're mastering your identity and starting your healing journey. As you continue learning about who you are, you may begin to see how your self-worth and self-esteem reflect on how you perceive yourself. Your experiences contribute to these perceptions. As Xuan, MJ, Star, Hana, and Nicole recount their stories, think about how you feel about your self-worth.

Xuan:

The summer between freshman and sophomore year, this guy from literature class invited me to a wedding. He was on the football team so you can imagine my reaction. We had a great time all summer, even called him my boyfriend, but his grandmother made it very clear she didn't want us dating because of my race. So, before the next school year, he said he didn't want to be tied down and we stopped seeing each other. Shortly after, I saw him with another girl. She was white, with blond hair and blue eyes. For a while, I felt undeserving or not beautiful enough because of my Asian features. It took a while to let that go.

MJ:

By the time I found out he was married, I had trichomonas, three abortions, and a child he didn't claim. It still hurts to this day when I think about it.

He told me lots of things over the years that I wanted to believe, so I just never looked anything up. I trusted every word he said to me. I saw him as a mentor. Someone I could learn from. Someone who could love me the way my parents couldn't. One summer after having our daughter, I found out he gave me my first sexually transmitted infection, but I continued dealing with him. I guess I thought he was as good as I could get.

Star:

I knew the relationship wasn't for me, but I tried to make it work and give her what she deserved. She was always stable and permanent, and it scared me so I started cheating on her. I had sex with other people (men and women) that I didn't like, and I knew didn't like me. I fell hard for other people and she still stayed. I had become addicted to toxic relationships and she was not that. Even now, I still have sex with people who only call me at three in the morning. I hook up with men who I'd never want to be seen with during the day, and I'm okay with it. I don't mind it because it's what I know. It's what I'm used to. Maybe it's what I deserve.

Hana:

A month later, he came to my house for the first time to work on a caseload. I had already ended the relationship I was in because I wanted more than my boyfriend was willing to give. When my newfound lover talked about his family, it made me want him more, seeing how committed he was to a relationship. That night, we had sex for the first time. After that, it seemed just physical for a while. He said he started developing feelings and I agreed, but neither one of us wanted to end what we were doing. I said I loved him first and told him he didn't have to say it back if he didn't want to. He didn't say it back that day and I wasn't upset because it wasn't something I needed to hear at the time. He talked about growing up alone and not feeling like he was ever supported by other people. He said I gave him that support and I believed him.

Nicole:

I had a history of depression, so I knew I would need help after realizing my ideas of a relationship were unhealthy. I struggled a lot with my anger, my insecurities, my disappointments, and all the other emotions that had held me back all of my life. It wasn't until they had boiled over in the form of alcohol abuse and suicide attempts, that I realized it was time for therapy. It wasn't just to benefit me, it was for my daughter too. She remembered my drunken nights of partying the pain away, and she remembered meeting mommy's new friend after friend; watching them go just as often as they'd come. My baby girl didn't believe my words when I said I was never drinking again. She soaked up my apologies like an over-used sponge. I would look in her eyes and know that she had grown tired of the "I'm sorry baby's" and of me, so to right my wrongs, I decided to go to therapy.

Step 3 - Activity

Self-worth is very hard for some people to identify or even measure.

You may wonder, "Is it how I perceive myself? Do my actions determine my self-worth? Or is it based on how others have treated me?"

Long story short, YOU determine your self-worth and how it's measured. Although this is an important step in the self-identity process, it can change as you evolve and redefine what you will tolerate. The main thing to remember is that you hold the power, so don't let anyone take that away from you. Never forget this, as there will be people who will try to tell you otherwise.

Part 1:

Look in the mirror and ask your reflection about who she is. Look at your reflection and say, I am worthy of

_____

_____

_____

_____

_____ (State one thing you are worthy of). Then finish the following sentence. "I am worthy because I _____

_____

_____

_____

_____, and I won't
commite to anyone who won't accept my worth."

Now write this again, and again, using different things you are
worthy of. Do this several times in the space provided at the
end of Part 3.

Never stop listening to your reflection. She is the most
vulnerable part of you and you need to hear her speak.

Part 2:

Once you have a good number of these responses, reflect on
what it looks like to accept yourself. What type of person
would someone need to be? Would they need to be kind,
understanding, and patient? Would they need to be
knowledgeable and accept your qualities? This is your time to
say what you mean. Own the things you want. Speak your
worth into existence and don't take anything that shows you
otherwise.

Part 3:

Mark this page in your book so that you can refer to this
exercise on a regular basis. You will need this when life gets
rough and when those around you try to determine your worth
for you.

Look at your reflection and say, I am worthy of

_____

_____

_____

_____ (State one thing you are worthy of). Then finish the following sentence. "I am worthy because I _____

_____

_____

_____, and I won't commit to anyone who won't accept my worth."

Look at your reflection and say, I am worthy of

_____

_____

_____

_____ (State one thing you are worthy of). Then finish the following sentence. "I am worthy because I _____

_____

_____

_____, and I won't commit to anyone who won't accept my worth."

Look at your reflection and say, I am worthy of

_____

_____

_____

_____

_____ (State one thing you are worthy of). Then finish the
following sentence. "I am worthy because I _____

_____

_____

_____

_____, and I won't
commit to anyone who won't accept my worth."

Look at your reflection and say, I am worthy of

_____

_____

_____

_____

_____ (State one thing you are worthy of). Then finish the
following sentence. "I am worthy because I _____

_____

_____

_____

_____, and I won't
commit to anyone who won't accept my worth."

Step 4: Build a Circle of Support

Write down how you're feeling so far. It can be about the things that are happening in your life right now or what you want to happen in the future. It can be specific or just a general thought. The best way to clear your mind is by expressing it and sharing your thoughts.

_____

_____

_____

_____

_____

_____

_____

_____

_____

_____

_____

_____

Next, you're going to learn how to pick the people to share your thoughts with. This step will take time as you navigate through building and rebuilding relationships. If someone is "toxic" and they just bring you down or never have anything good to say about you, tell them how you feel. You will read how the women in this step dealt with the people around them, and how they surrounded themselves with people who championed for their successes.

Tesia:

There was this girl I used to talk to. We were friends that were occasionally in touch for a few years—about every six months or so. She called me one day to pick her up from the hospital. She just had a baby and wanted to give it away 'cause she was on drugs. There was a baby crib in her room but no baby in it. She was talking to a white woman who introduced herself as an adoption counselor or something. I was shocked cause I didn't know the girl was even pregnant. I said, "Ma'am, you can leave. We're not putting any more black babies in the system." The lady laughed and continued talking to my friend. This woman was giving my friend options on adoption and foster care when neither of them had even seen the baby yet. My friend told me she was just going to have the baby and leave but something happened and she had to stay an extra day for observation. That was why she called me. I convinced her to see her baby for the first time, hoping it would change her mind, but I could tell there was no connection. I remember my friend saying to the baby, "You're cute but I can't keep you," and there were no tears in her eyes when she said it. Just emptiness. I told her I would keep the baby for a while until she was ready to be a mom.

Learning how to be a caregiver came pretty natural to me. I had all of my family to support me too. At the time I was still living with my parents, and although my dad would rotate changing and feeding shifts at night, it was my mom who helped the most. I even had my grandparents babysitting her sometimes. My family had my back.

Star:

I was around fourteen or fifteen when I started going to a place called The Attic for "at-risk" youth. That's where I found people I could call family. None of us had much of a home to go to but we kinda had each other.

It was my family who put money in a pot and bailed me out of jail. I didn't know that my family even knew where I was until a C.O. told me I had money in my commissary. It felt like the gates of heaven had opened. The next day, another C.O. said to me, "Carter, wrap it up". That's when I knew I was going home. They didn't even tell me who was picking me up, and I didn't care. As I walked out, I saw my niece and sister right there waiting for me.

Step 4 - Activity

Did any of these stories resonate with you? Did anything stand out that you can take from?

_____

_____

_____

_____

_____

_____

_____

_____

_____

_____

_____

_____

_____

_____

Jawana, Star, and Tesia put the people around them to a test without knowing it. They challenged friends, family, and others to support them when things were uncomfortable. For instance, Tesia made a decision to care for a child she had not planned on raising. It was a life-altering event that Tesia would need support to get through. Without her family, her decisions may have been different. Because the people around Tesia believed in her, they were able to support her. Those are the type of circles you want to be surrounded by. People who see the greatness you are capable of and support you along your journey.

Part 1:

What is support? What does it look like? How do you measure it? Look up "support" in the dictionary and write your response below.

_____

_____

_____

_____

_____

_____

_____

Find synonyms for the word "support." Once you find them, write them down.

_____

_____

_____

_____

_____

_____

Part 2:

Support can come from any part of your life. It can be a group on social media, family members, friends, strangers, your therapist, church members, or your children. The support can be financial, spiritual, psychological, or health-related, to name a few. Support can also come in the form of wisdom, or education you didn't have, the ability to speak about your emotions, a place to stay, a shoulder to cry on, forgiveness, and patience. Make sure that the support you receive is not conditional upon sex, control, isolation from others, or participating in acts that you don't agree with.

Do you have a circle of support?   YES   NO

If you said yes, who are they? Do you know the ways in which they have shown you support? Feel free to write down as many people as you need to, that you feel truly support you. If you don't have a phone number for them, GET ONE.

Name: Support: Phone #:	Name: Support: Phone #:
Name: Support: Phone #:	Name: Support: Phone #:
Name: Support: Phone #:	Name: Support: Phone #:
Name: Support: Phone #:	Name: Support: Phone #:

Now that you have verified or identified your circle of support, attach pictures of people who support you. You can put your photos on a wall or in this very book. You will refer to them when you are at your lowest. This will help you see that you have them in your life and that you are not alone.

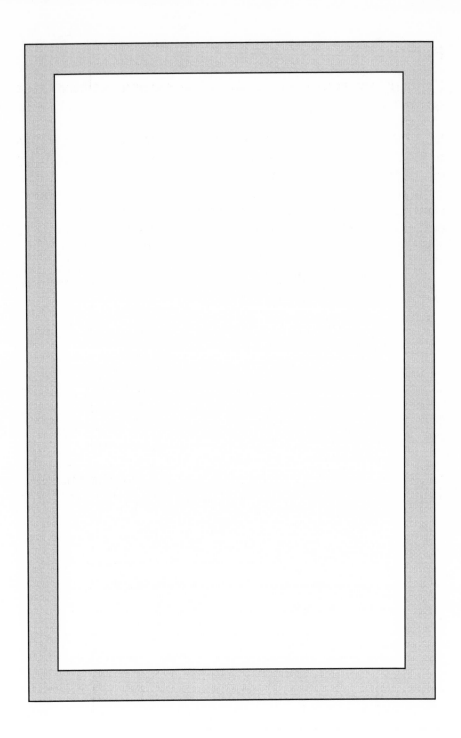

Part 3:

If you're not sure whether you have support, answer these questions:

Who can I call when I'm in trouble? Who can I trust to be honest with me? Do I have someone to encourage me, help me heal, and bring positivity?

If you don't have a circle of support yet, don't worry it will come, so be ready. Begin figuring out what that support looks like and how you can reciprocate it. Most importantly, don't confuse support with dependency. Support builds self-sufficiency and freedom. Dependency is a form of support that can manifest into restriction of freedom.

Part 4:

Once you've established your circle, start spending time with them. Get to know them, do things with them. Go on trips, have movie nights, go dancing, or just keep each other company sometimes. Be sure to choose wisely as these should be the people who have your best interest at heart and have your back when you need them most. Oh! Don't forget to make sure this support is mutual. They need you just as much as you need them.

My thoughts: Today's Date: _____

_____

_____

_____

_____

_____

_____

_____

_____

Step 5: Protect Your Mind

Your mind is full of thoughts. When thoughts become actions, they are recorded as memories. If you're not careful, negative thoughts lead to negative actions and painful memories. Protect your mind so no one can manipulate it. If you control your mind then you can maintain power over your actions. Pay close attention to what can happen when you don't protect it and what can happen when you do.

Jawana:

I tried to get back on track with my dreams. I knew I wanted to go and was adamant about leaving, but he begged me to stay since money was tight for him.

I didn't want to be there, so I left mentally first. Then I started cutting him off financially. I always had my own money, so it was nothing to stay in hotels until I figured out a plan. This was me fighting for myself. Fighting for my own sanity.

Xuan:

After my high school boyfriend, I entered every relationship expecting to be abandoned. To protect myself, I created deal-breakers; which meant that if certain standards were not met, the person didn't have a chance. And although I had long-lasting relationships, the guy always seemed to possess a quality or behavior that didn't match my standards. I had only four deal breakers but I lived by them: infidelity, financial instability, political and social prejudices, and being a deadbeat. I told myself I was going to be smart next time.

If you listen closely to Xuan and Jawana, you will hear them say they took their experiences and used them to learn and grow. Their minds were able to act as their first defense against manipulation. It is important to understand that if not addressed, these experiences become patterns of familiarity. You have to program your mind to break cycles manipulation in order to stop them from manifesting.

Step 5 - Activity

Inside the following circle, write a few of your happiest and most positive thoughts about yourself (you can refer to Step 1 if you need to).

Then, in the large space outside of the circle, write some things people have said or done to try and break that wall of happiness.

Along the outside of the circle, between your thoughts and other's thoughts about you, write how you can protect your happiness. You can use your responses in Step 3, on Self-Worth, or you can include those from your circle of support. For example, Xuan created standards to protect herself from future disappointment.

OTHER PEOPLE'S THOUGHTS
ABOUT ME

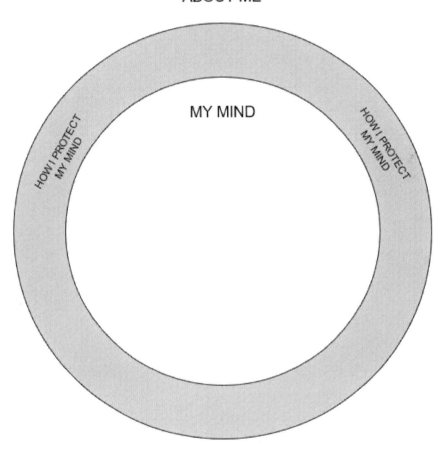

My thoughts:

_____

_____

_____

_____

_____

_____

_____

_____

_____

_____

_____

_____

_____

_____

_____

_____

_____

_____

_____

_____

_____

_____

_____

_____

_____

Step 6: Protect Your Body

Star, MJ, and Jawana are about to share some of their most personal experiences in this step. They have done this for you, so listen and learn.

Star:

This chick I met before Laree liked to fight me and it was basically because I didn't accept the things she told me. I gave her all of me and I hoped she was going to do the same. But really, I think I knew better. People only do what you let them do. I let her hurt me because I believed that was what love felt like.

MJ:

A few weeks after having my daughter, I had severe cramping and was taken to the hospital, where an emotionless nurse told me that I had trichomonas. After she told me, she walked out of the emergency room and left me to process it alone. I had no clue what it was or what it meant. I was given an antibiotic, some information on preventative care, and sent on my way. I called my daughter's father as soon as I got home—tears streaming down my face. First, he told me that the doctors didn't really know where it came from. Then, he claimed he was in front of a computer looking it up and found that dirty swimming pools could cause it as well. I was a lifeguard at the time, so it kinda made sense. I never questioned it again. I know better now.

Jawana:

He grabbed me. Digging his hands into my face, he picked me up by my head, and threw me to the ground. I hit the concrete face-first. I went in and out of consciousness as he towered over me, palming my head and banging it into the ground. I remember mumbling that my phone was cracked, and everything was blurry after that.

Step 6 - Activity

Part 1:

Think about these questions: What did I just read? What about these stories stood out to me? How did I feel hearing them? Did any of them reflect some of my own struggles with protecting my body?

Write about a time your body had no protection, and what happened?

_____

_____

_____

_____

_____

_____

_____

_____

_____

_____

_____

_____

Part 2:

Inside the following circle, name your most important parts of your body and why they're so important to you. Along the outside of the circle, write down how you can protect those parts. You can also include individuals from your circle of support as protection.

OTHER PEOPLE'S THOUGHTS
ABOUT MY BODY

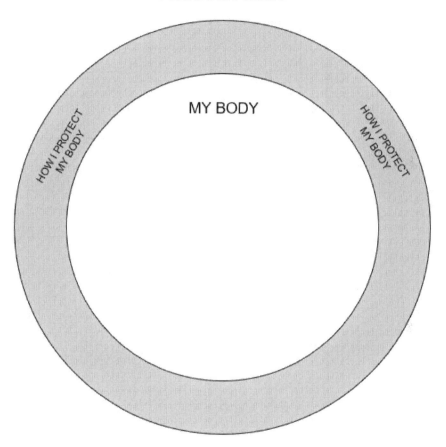

I hope you feel stronger after this exercise, because you are stronger, and will continue to grow stronger the more you find your power.

My thoughts:

_____

_____

_____

_____

_____

_____

_____

_____

_____

_____

_____

_____

_____

_____

_____

_____

_____

_____

_____

_____

_____

_____

_____

_____

_____

_____

_____

Step 7: Protect Your Spirit

Star:

I started living in foster care when I was eleven. Surprisingly, nothing traumatizing or even bad happened to me during my early years in foster care. In fact, that's where I first learned about God.

Jawana:

When the cops arrested me, they had to take me to the hospital before sending me to jail. The judge reduced my bail bond, but I still couldn't get out because I couldn't call anyone. I didn't know anyone else in the state, so I sat in jail for a month and a half. While I was in there, I read the bible, talked to other women, and realized I was done with the bullshit.

Sarah:

Letting it go was the best thing I could have done. By praying and giving it to God, I was able to heal and move on because I kept my spirit clean. And sometimes that meant being able to forgive.

MJ:

I go to Thai Chi in the mornings. It's the meditation part that I like the most. My teacher is this old Chinese man who only knows how to say hello in my language but that's okay. When we start class, everyone is silent. It's like only our spirits are talking. It's the most amazing feeling in the world.

Step 7 - Activity

Inside the following circle, write down everything that your spirit is or represents. Is it your love? Is it your spiritual beliefs? Is it your morals? Outside of the circle, write down how you can protect your spirit. You can refer back to Step 1 as a reference to what you believe in.

OTHER PEOPLE'S THOUGHTS
ABOUT MY SPIRIT

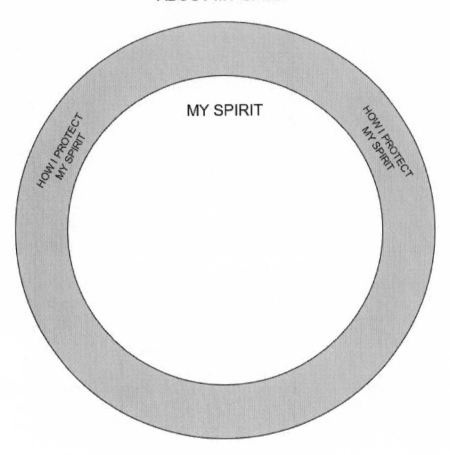

Your spirit is precious, you may want to add layers of protection around it, once you've developed your foundation. Never forget to protect your spirit no matter what.

Step 8: Putting It All Together

Part 1: Mind

There are a few ways that you can protect your mind. One way is through knowledge—knowledge of self and of your environment. You learn this in different ways, through different sources, and with different perspectives. Since you have begun to discover your identity and develop your self-worth, take some time now to look up articles, read case studies, watch documentaries, and ask around to see what others have to say about subjects that matter to you. Apply what you've learned about yourself to the world around you. Have your views changed? Consider how those views impacted your relationships when you think of the people in your circle. How do your views differ? How are they similar? Remember, your mind is yours to protect—make sure it's sharp.

Part 2: Body

Your body holds your mind. What affects your body will affect your mind. Star didn't realize it, but every time she had sex with someone or let them cause her physical harm, she let them have a say in her worth. She was physically degraded so often that she began to treat herself the same way those people treated her.

Think of the people you let into your life.

How many are lovers? _____

Out of that number, how often do you wear protection? _____

How many times do you get into a disagreement that leads to a physical altercation? _____

Are you concerned about contracting an STD? _____

When, if ever, was the last time you had sex with someone because they paid, forced or manipulated you into doing so?

_____

_____

_____

_____

_____

_____

_____

_____

_____

_____

Find a mirror. Look at that woman or girl, who was violated and acknowledge her. Acknowledge how she felt in those moments. Understand that it wasn't her fault.

~ TAKE A DEEP BREATH ~

Unpack everything you're feeling right now.

_____

_____

_____

_____

_____

_____

_____

_____

_____

_____

_____

_____

_____

_____

_____

_____

_____

_____

_____

_____

_____

_____

_____

_____

_____

_____

~ YOU ARE NOT ALONE ~

No matter what has happened, you now have support. Always talk to someone within your circle.

Your body is just as precious as your mind and your spirit. And in many beliefs, they are the same. Start asking questions for the answers you want to know: for example, have they ever had a sexually transmitted disease or what their sexual orientation is. Next, ask yourself if their answers make sense. Remember, you want to protect your body the same way you protect your thoughts.

These questions may seem embarrassing to ask, but you still have to ask them. Those who want to hurt you will plan on you being too afraid to ask them. Don't forget: If it doesn't feel right, sound right, or look right—IT ISN'T. Listen to your warning signs and stay away.

Part 3: Spirit

Start figuring out what you believe in. Ask yourself these questions: What do I believe in? Why do I believe in this? What are the principles of this beliefs? Do these principles fit with my lifestyle, morals, or values? Why or why not? Am I willing to change my lifestyle or values for this belief?

Once you've figured out what your spirituality is, begin to see if the people who come into your life know or understand this about you. Start asking questions about how they see your beliefs. Ask them about theirs as well. It is important to note that you are only asking others this to weed out those who want to dominate or control your spirit. You can always make adjustments or completely change your beliefs, but it should be on your terms. You shouldn't be afraid to say what you believe in around people who truly care about you.

Step 8 - Activity

Below, fill your circles and the spaces outside of them as you have in steps 5, 6, and 7. Try to blend those thoughts and feelings with one another. Your three individual parts all connect and build on each other. If you harbor bad thoughts within your mind, they will affect how you take care of your spirit and how you will treat your body. Give them all equal care and love.

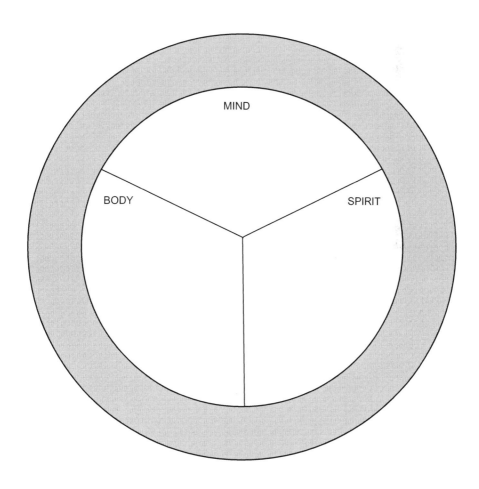

My thoughts:

Step 9: Set Goals

Goals can change and are ever reaching. The wonderful thing about goals is that you get to set them. This step is important because so many times we get so wrapped in our daily lives that we forget to look at the bigger picture— "Why am I doing this?" Tesia, MJ, Jene, and Sarah won't let life stop them from their goals. Even if you don't reach your goals right away, think about the poem by Gracie Allen that emphasizes the importance of not giving up too soon. Now, listen and learn what setting goals can look and feel like so that you are able to accomplish any goal that you set your mind to.

Tesia:

The goal was to adopt this precious little girl as my daughter. It was a long process that her mother refused to go through. I think the courts saw that I was more invested in this child than her biological mother, which is why I was awarded guardianship. I had to pass a background check, the house safety check, and I had to prove there was an established relationship between me and the biological mother. I wasn't sure that would be enough, but it was. I was finally able to bring her home as my daughter after passing a car seat safety class. It's still can't believe that I got through the process, but I did because I didn't give up.

MJ:

Before I knew it, the weeks turned into months, and the months turned into years. Therapy for me was meditation. It kept me calm, centered, and at peace with myself and everything around me. I hadn't realized it then, but therapy helped me become a better me. I still have my hiccups from time to time, but my goal to just get better outweighs all the mistakes.

Jene:

It wasn't until my second attempt at high school that I even thought about attending college. I never thought my book smarts would get me past high school, until I was accepted to college through the City Year program. The fall after getting my high school diploma, I was attending a university. It was overwhelming for me as a teen, but I enjoyed it. It was a place I could thrive and I didn't want it to end—not without a degree. My freshman year, I had to put my education on hold for the sake of my new family. It was a decision I would always remember.

I remember the day I went back to college for the second time, as a mother of three. I guess two times is a charm for me. It was a surreal feeling and I felt at home, but there was also a reluctance. Did I belong there? Would I be able to finish a two-year program? Would I still be able to give my children the attention they needed? These questions ran through my mind often in the beginning. However, those thoughts wouldn't stop me from my goals, and they didn't. Decades later, I would walk down the aisle of Strayer University's graduation ceremony with my Master's Degree in Business. It took a while, but I never gave up.

Sarah:

We stayed with his parents for two years until he finished build'n our home. When it was complete, we stayed in that home until we moved to Philadelphia around 1968. We had one child and then twins several years later—all boys. I still try to imagine what life would have been like had he just given up on build'n that house and work'n to save money. Women didn't have much to do durin' those days 'cept tendn' to the children, but I still found a way to work at a sewing factory to help save up. Things weren't perfect durin' those times, especially not for coloreds, but we loved each other and I knew how much taking care of his family meant to him.

Step 9 - Activity

Let's take a look at Jene. She is now a working professional who holds a Master's Degree in Business, and when she isn't working, she's traveling with her sorority sisters and close friends. She does this, all while being an active mother and grandmother, "Nana" as she calls herself. What's fascinating about Jene is that she began her journey with little hope of making it out of her circumstances. Against all odds, Jene worked toward her goals. And no matter who she met or what she went through, she was determined to reach them. Although she dropped out of high school, she motivated herself to earn her high school diploma. When she left college to get married and grow her family, Jene knew she'd return and that's exactly what she prepared her mind for. She created goals and set out to achieve them.

Part 1:

Think of a time when you wanted to complete something but life kept getting in the way.

How did it make you feel?

_____

_____

_____

_____

_____

_____

_____

_____

_____

_____

_____

Did you take a break from it?

_____

_____

Did you eventually complete it?

_____

_____

Did you have support?

_____

_____

Are you still trying to complete it?

_____

_____

Do you have support now? If so, Who?

_____

_____

All of these questions will help determine if you are serious about reaching the goals you've set. Your motivation has to come from within, and your circle of support will be there in many different ways. But first, you have to want it—no matter what.

Part 2:

On the next page, write a list of short and long-term goals that you want to accomplish within the next five years. Whether you set a goal to have lots of children, get the job of your dreams or publish your first book, list them here.

0-2 YEAR GOAL LIST	3-5 YEAR GOAL LIST

Part 3:

Once you have reached your goal, check it off. Be sure to put the date. You will appreciate those dates as you look back.

Even if you have to push the goal post, don't forget, these are your goals and they can be modified or changed as necessary. What matters is that you never stop pushing toward the goals you set. With this mindset, you will reach your goals.

Part 4:

Collect a few magazines, print out some pictures, and/or gather photos of things related to your goals. On the next page, create a collage of dreams and goals you wish to accomplish using the images you have collected.

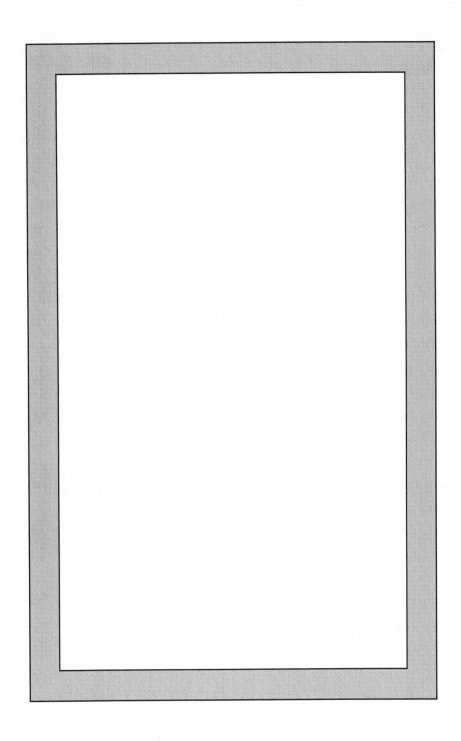

Step 10: Make Room for Love

Sometimes, our heartache can be so severe that we stop loving. I'm here to tell you, don't stop loving yourself or others. Don't give up on love. Instead, redefine what love looks and feels like based on your experiences. Remember to love YOU first. After you have established love within yourself, be cautious about who you give your love to. It's okay to be patient when it comes to giving it out, but always continue to love.

Hello queen! I'm so proud that you've made it this far. I know that by now, you've taken great strides as we have passed this book's midway point. I want to share some extra words for you to build on.

As a child, I thought I was unloved. Those feelings would make me physically and emotionally harm myself—even when I wasn't aware of it. My thoughts were negative, my mind was negative, my actions were negative and my heart was like spoiled fruit. I blamed everyone around me, including myself, for my pain and misery.

One day, I looked within ME and realized that in order to heal my heart, I had to nurture that piece of withered fruit, nourish my good thoughts and purify my mind with inner peace and self-love. I began to love who I was and check in on my feelings regularly. Over time, that bitter fruit in me became sweet wine. But it wasn't easy.

I had to learn that I was not alone in this world or with my experiences, and that is what helped me understand the process of loving. I found true love when I finally loved me.

Step 10 - Activity

What is love to you? What does this concept mean? How do you see it? How do you feel it? Write down the answers to these questions. Write in as much detail as you need to. Your responses will be the prototype for who you open up to and who you share your mind, body, and spirit with. Your love is very precious and should be given with care.

_____

_____

_____

_____

_____

_____

_____

_____

_____

_____

_____

_____

_____

_____

_____

_____

_____

Once you identify what your understanding of love looks like, you'll be able to see when someone is not loving you; as they will show you contradictory behaviors. These behaviors signal RED FLAGS, which we'll discuss in the next step.

Step 11: Address the Red Flags

Have you ever learned something about someone that made the hair on the back of your neck stand up? Did you ever notice that the behavior of a person you were spending time with made you feel uncomfortable? Well, those were all warning signs telling you that something wasn't right, and your brain alerted the rest of your body to pay attention.

For instance, you are with a new friend who invites you to his house and tells you it will be just you and him, but as you get closer to the house you hear multiple cheers from male voices. Your mind starts paying attention to distinct sounds to validate the friend's story. Once the story and supporting evidence don't match, your mind sends out signals. In this book, these signals are defined as RED FLAGS.

As you read the following stories, see if you notice any RED FLAGS in Hana, Jawana, and Tesia's experiences that indicate something isn't right.

Hana:

Before we became lovers, he was in, what he called, a 20-year relationship. So, when this handsome man asked me if I was single, I proudly told him I was in an open situation myself. He asked me if I would consider sleeping with him because he wasn't happy. As we got to know each other, we began flirting more. We even started going out to dinner, but he wouldn't hold my hand in public. I wanted to, but I also understood.

He was upset with me after finding out that I had told his family members about how I felt, and his 'fiancé' started harassing me on social media. Things started getting complicated after he started inviting me to family gatherings and I began to build relationships with them. That's when his cousin confessed to me that they were actually married, had been cheating on each other throughout their 20 years together, and that they had no intentions of divorcing because of their three kids.

MJ:

I met my daughter's father when I was fourteen, on my way to the Papi store at the end of my street. He was 28 at the time. He told me he liked my lips, and asked for my phone number. I gave it to him—kinda, because I changed the last digit. I guess he knew that trick because he still reached me that night. He said he couldn't pick me up in front of my house. I thought it was odd, but didn't want to seem too scared. We drove around until we made our way to a hotel on the other side of town. I was still nervous, but I didn't know how to say it. After sex, we ordered food and laid in the bed together. I still remember what it felt like to lay in his arms, because this was the part I longed for—the kisses and the hugging made me feel special. When we woke up, the sun was almost up. He rushed me out and dropped me off a block away from my house. I walked home ashamed yet satisfied. That would be our routine for the next two years.

Tesia:

I met my adopted daughter's biological dad once, but it was brief. My daughter's biological mother hesitantly set it up, and he didn't seem interested at all. My daughter's biological mom said she wanted to get herself together so she could regain custody. Instead of getting herself together, she kept doing drugs and missing court hearings. She wouldn't show up to visit the very child she gave birth to, and never took the parenting classes like she said she would.

Salina:

Being pregnant with my first daughter at fourteen and giving birth at fifteen was terrifying. I told the guy who got me pregnant about it when I first found out, and he told me to get an abortion. I couldn't, because I was already two months along. When I decided to keep the baby, he didn't really want other people to know about it or us. When we were together, he wanted to be involved, but when he was around people that he knew, it was like he didn't want anything to do with us.

Jene:

Imagine being a 17-year-old high school dropout in your first serious relationship. I didn't have many relationships before that so when a charming 24-year-old man gave me more attention than I knew how to handle, I decided to build my family with him. Like any naive girl in love, I dropped out of college, got married, and spent seven years working different jobs to help put food on the table. I realized later that my then-husband just wanted me to be a housewife while he chased his ever-changing ambitions.

Star:

He started asking me if I wanted to try drugs, the kind I knew to stay away from. Then he started doing them in front of me. Eventually, I started trying them too. Before I knew it, we were getting high together and I think that's what he wanted.

Jawana:

We were at the grocery store and we had different cereal choices—I wanted Raisin Bran, and he wanted Cinnamon Toast Crunch. I started complaining about not wanting the same thing he wanted. Then, out of nowhere, he smacked the cereal out my hand. I think I said something to provoke him, 'cause he punched me in my face and walked off. The hit turned into a black eye and he apologized non-stop. My friends asked me if they could beat him up, but I said no—I forgave and forgot what he did until it happened again.

Step 11: Activity

RED FLAGS are warnings and can be experienced in many ways. For example, a red flag can be intuition, an admission, or evidence. These red flags go against the values you have set for yourself and those that come into your life.

In this list, write down behaviors that you would consider deal breakers or things that go against your values and well-being, then we'll talk about why this is important.

DEAL BREAKERS	RED FLAG
Example: Dating married men	*Example: Wedding band on left ring finger*

Being able to identify red flags will help you organize your next course of action upon your discovery. In some cases, you may have to do some research to confirm your intuition. Step 12 of this book will discuss the importance of conducting research.

Now, create a plan for what to do next. Will you present your feelings or evidence to the person? What happens if they call you crazy or insecure? What happens if they admit what they've done? What will you do if children are involved? What if they have a temper? You have to be willing to put your own heart and mind first, even if that means walking away from a long-term or developing relationship. You must draw a hard line for when enough will be enough and stick to your guns. Most importantly, inform members within your circle of support of your next course of action.

Always reach out to your circle of support established in Step 4 if you are not sure what to do. They will act as your eyes, ears, and voice of reason to protect you from harm.

Was there ever a time when you felt like something wasn't quite right? Did you act on those feelings? What was the outcome?

All of those feelings represent your intuition. Describe what your intuition felt like. How did your body react to those feelings of intuition?

_____

_____

_____

_____

_____

_____

_____

_____

_____

_____

_____

_____

Step 12: Do Your Research

You have now identified your deal breakers, and you are able to identify the warning signs that tell you something is not right. So what's next? This step is all about research. This step will show you how to begin research on the people you meet.

Oh, before I forget—you should be doing some form of research on EVERYONE you meet. Whether it is the friendly yoga girl who invites you to coffee, or the guy at the supermarket who wants to take you out to dinner. Step 4 taught you that your circle of support should be filled with those who bring positivity to your life no matter who they are. Be sure to refer back to Step 4 regularly, to reference what healthy relationships should look and feel like.

Hana:

After many wasted months, I finally realized the man I loved was an asshole. Although he told me he was in a relationship, the extent of it was not communicated. It wasn't until after the drama, that I realized I never had a chance of being more than a side chick.

MJ:

Years after being tired of his lies, I got the sense to look up Trichomonas, "the pool infection", that he told me was normal for a swimmer. I found out it was actually what the doctors said it was, a sexually transmitted infection.

I decided to take pictures from his house to get the names of the children he denied having. I memorized the "plaintiff's" name on a piece of mail that read, "Child Support Services". That's how I found out he had more than just two children. I googled his name in my local public records database and found a marriage license attached to as well.

One morning after sex, I realized I didn't need any more evidence to convince myself he was never going to change. He offered to take me home, so as I walked to the front door, I took a quick glance around his cluttered living room. I remember seeing the television I tried to smash when he attempted to hide me from another woman. I remember mountains of clothes hiding child support orders, women's jewelry, and condoms. I scanned that house that I'd lain in the night before and knew I could never come back. It was clear the child I had with him would suffer and it would be my fault. I wish the 14-year-old me knew what I know now.

Jawana:

All the behaviors I thought were weird or off started to add up. I began applying this sixth sense to other people I met. I started paying more attention to details and looking into things a bit more when things didn't feel right.

What do you think of the experiences of these three women? How did they make you feel? Think about what you've learned so far.

The activity on the next page will help you with conducting research as well as provide available public resources to get started.

Step 12 - Activity

Part 1:

Write down the names of your five most recent partner(s) and by each name, I want you to write as much information as you can remember about them. For example, what was their full name? Who did they live with? How old were they? When was their last relationship, or were they ever married? Did they have siblings or children? Where did they work? Where did they go to school? How many people had they been with prior to you? Were their partners male or female?

Name: What I know about this person:
Name: What I know about this person:
Name: What I know about this person:
Name: What I know about this person:
Name: What I know about this person:

Once you have written down all the information you can recall, write down what you wish you could have known that you didn't find out until later in the relationship or encounter.

Name: What I wish I knew about this person:
Name: What I wish I knew about this person:
Name: What I wish I knew about this person:
Name: What I wish I knew about this person:
Name: What I wish I knew about this person:

Part 2:

Use the information you wish you could've known as a model for what you want to know about the next person you meet. Do this before becoming intimate. If they can't wait, that should be a red flag.

Fill in the information of any new person you are thinking about becoming intimate with. Use the research tools in the next activity to verify information, and be sure to go over this information with someone in your circle of support.

Name: What I know about this person:
Name: What I know about this person:
Name: What I know about this person:
Name: What I know about this person:
Name: What I know about this person:

It might feel a little imposing to do research on someone, but ALWAYS remember this is for your safety. This is for your protection. This is for your younger self. Show her that you have grown.

Part 3:

Keep applying this step to each person who enters your life. Take any information this new person has given you and compare it to what you find out about them. For example, if they say they are not married, simply type their full name into public records under "marriage license" to verify this. You will need their date of birth and full name, which is why gathering information is so important. If they say their last name is Reed, confirm this with some form of identification or photo ID. Then look their first and last name up on social media platforms to see their views and how they interact with others online. If they say they own a business, look it up on the Better Business Bureau's website. And yes, this is all public record. You won't have to spend any money on this type of research.

This may feel like a lot of work or feel too intrusive. Fight those feelings. All you're doing is verifying what they have told you. If they told you they were away at college for five years, but you find out they have been in prison—that should be a red flag.

Research Starting Points	Social Media Research Starting Points
National Sex Offenders Registry Better Business Bureau: BBB.org Census information: Census.gov	Facebook Instagram Twitter LinkedIn

Although social media sites are ever-changing, information about people on public platforms continues to grow. Social media will be the best type of research for new and updated information about the people you meet.

Step 13: Overcome the Need to Settle

Can you recall a time when you settled for something or someone that wasn't right for you? Well, this step is a glimpse of Jawana, Jene, and Sarah's experiences: two of which are cautionary, of how they learned to stop settling.

Jawana:

My sister introduced us since she knew him and I was single, but I didn't think he was on my level. Somehow, he became a friend and he just grew on me. We moved to another state together, and that was around the time he began to change.

When we moved back to Atlanta, he went to trade school, but they found out he didn't get his high school diploma, so two weeks into classes they kicked him out. He started arguing with me, telling me I acted like I was better than him. The truth is, I did feel that way. I called him dumb and it turned into a fight. He pushed me and I pushed him back once or twice. He pulled my hair and slammed my head into a mirror on the floor, like a basketball. I told him to go shit on his-self since I knew about his medical condition, and called him a "crippled ass motha fucker". I regret saying it now but my words were the power my arms weren't. I would go in on him; calling him all types of names, but it made things worse. I didn't tell anyone about the abuse because he was crippled, and I didn't think I was in an abusive relationship at the time.

Jene:

One day I looked up, and I was still in a situation that barely paid the bills. I was watching the people around me get promoted after only being on the job a short time because their degree, and I understood what I needed to do to move up. So, I picked the school I wanted to attend and I applied. My husband wanted me to stay home and take care of the kids, but I was tired of struggling.

Sarah:

When I met Clifton, Butch as we called him, he was a grade· behind me. We went to school together up to high school. Summertime came, and we worked for the same white man on the farm to pick cotton, chop grass, stack hay, and do all other farm work. We kept being in each other's company until we got to be sixteen years old, and he asked to be my boyfriend. I went to his father's store, pass'n four stores just to see him. He had his ways but he treated me special. At eighteen, we asked our parents if we could get married, but they said no. So we went to Dillon, South Carolina and got married on our own. We were married for 43 years until death parted us.

Sarah knew what she wanted, and who she wanted it with. She didn't settle for anything else. She went with her gut and followed her heart. As you go through this book, I understand it can seem overwhelming. But don't get discouraged. These steps are to get you ready—to prepare you for long-lasting love. Nothing is or will be perfect. However, the goal is to love yourself and be at peace despite what you go through.

Step 13 - Activity

Jawana went through severe physical and mental abuse by her then-boyfriend even after recognizing the red flags because she doubted her self-worth. Jawana didn't have a book like the one you're reading right now to help her. She didn't know she had an immediate circle of support either. So Jawana decided to give a piece of herself to someone who didn't deserve it. Had this queen taken her time to assess her self-worth and establish goals, she may have never settled.

Part 1:

Similar to what you have done for Step 3 on self-worth, write down a list of expectations on what you want to see from the people you meet. For example, would you like them to be employed? Do you prefer that they don't smoke? Maybe, you'd expect them to have a college degree.

Give yourself time to think about what type of qualities you would like to see. Once you have created your list of expectations, think about past experiences where you set expectations regarding who you chose to spend your time with. What was the experience? How was it, were your expectations met?

_____

_____

_____

_____

_____

_____

_____

_____

_____

_____

_____

_____

_____

_____

_____

_____

_____

_____

Practice Time!!

My goals are _____

_____

_____

_____

_____.

The people who come into my life need to know these are my goals.

I want my next partner to be _____

_____

_____

_____

and to have _____

_____

_____

_____before meeting me, and to know how to

_____

_____

_____

_____. The person who comes into my life needs to know I have these expectations.

An example of positive support is _____

_____

_____

_____

The people who come into my life need to know this is what I recognize as positive support.

Part 2:

Now that you have your expectations, figure out which these expectations can be adjusted and for what reasons. Expectations are there to protect you, but sometimes, you will need to adjust them or at least compromise a little. Please be very careful with adjusting your expectations. Only adjust them when doing so will not cause you physical, emotional or psychological harm.

Part 3:

Go over your expectations regularly, as they will change during different stages of your growth.

You're almost there!

Step 14: Stick With It

If you are at this step, that means you have already found a form of therapy that works for you. If this is the case, then Nicole and Salina's stories will continue to give you hope and motivation to keep going. No matter how hard it gets, just remember that you now have the tools to find your happiness.

Nicole:

I met my partner about a year into my therapy. Telling him wasn't hard, because at that point I was proud of my journey and ready to find someone who could accept me for me. So, once we realized that we were going to be more than a one-night-stand that wouldn't go away, I told him about my therapy. After sharing our journeys, it seemed easier for us to get along and figure out what we wanted from one another.

Therapy gets me through the difficult moments, like the mental breakdowns and the traumas that resurface. It guides my emotions to healthy places, and helps create strategies when I have those difficult moments.

Salina:

I have been going to marriage counseling with my now husband, and I am learning that I never really thought about what my talents were or who or what I wanted to be in life. I got pregnant when I was so young, and never had time to experience self-love.

I have two daughters, and I want them to have time to learn about themselves before becoming mothers. Once a child comes, you are your last priority, and your child comes first.

Step 14 - Activity

Part 1:

Here is an opportunity for you to share your experience with your chosen therapy. Be honest and take your time when exploring your thoughts. We have come so far together, now it's time for you to unpack what you've been doing since you started this journey.

_____

_____

_____

_____

_____

_____

_____

_____

_____

_____

_____

_____

_____

_____

_____

_____

_____

_____

_____

_____

Part 2:

With your eyes closed, take a deep breath. As you breathe, think of all the things you call baggage. Think of your troubles and worries. Think of all your pain, embarrassments, insecurities, and mistakes.

Part 3:

Now that you have thought of all those, own them, claim them. These things reflect where you once were. They have changed as you've grown, and will continue to change as you continue to grow. When you inhale all that baggage, you are taking everything in. Your mind is sifting through that baggage as you inhale. At this moment, no one else is to blame for the things you need to work on, and no one is given credit for the things you have accomplished within yourself. For these few seconds, your baggage belongs to you—Good or Bad.

Part 4:

With your eyes closed, count to ten slowly and calmly.

Part 5:

Exhale. Let your baggage go, as you replace it with clean, new experiences. These experiences are what will make you shine uniquely in your skin. Love this woman you have become, because the moment you are able to let go of your baggage and love yourself, is the moment you make it easier for the people around you to love you. Your circle of support will grow, and your goals will be attainable. This is you, setting your soul free to find the love you have been looking for.

Step 15: Become Happily Single

Xuan:

People ask me why I'm still not married and have no children. I just tell them I have so much emotional love and support, that I'm okay. I love just being Aunty.

I worked on loving myself and staying away from men who didn't get it. I focused on my career and family, and before I knew it, ten years had gone by and somehow, I have never felt happier. I go on dates, but I come home to me and I enjoy that freedom. Sometimes it gets hard when I need to move something big or get my car fixed, because I don't have anyone to take care of those things for me. I call my friends and we struggle and laugh, and it feels amazing.

I'm not opposed to being with someone or even having children, but I don't want to be unhappy. I want to be in a situation that makes me smile when I think of it. My mom once told me that she had to grow into loving my dad because times were different. That's not something I ever want to have to do.

Sarah:

I didn't enjoy anything for years, until I started to go to senior events. My life changed and I started to forget. Maybe it was my way of healing.

Nicole:

I was single for years after I finally walked away. I started my business, and I was going out to different events. I went back to school, earned my degree, and my life started to feel like mine again. Now when I go out, my goal is not to find "the one," instead it's to meet new people and just get back to enjoying life—you know, letting the Universe guide me.

Step 15 - Activity

The best way to truly be happy is by knowing yourself, loving yourself, and enjoying the time you spend with YOU.

Part 1:

Get on your phone or computer and google "city events." After a little digging, you will find local groups, events, and activities to attend. Once you find some events you're interested in, add them to your calendar. If you find that two or more events overlap, add them all. It always feels good to have options. Feel free to use the calendar at the end of this activity.

Once you complete this activity, check the box ☐

Part 2:

After your first few events, write about your experiences. Think about how you felt in a new environment, did you meet any new people? Would you go to these events again, and what other activities would you like to try next?

_____

_____

_____

_____

_____

_____

_____

_____

_____

_____

_____

Part 3:

Once you begin doing things and going to places you enjoy, get to know the people in the spaces you frequent. Find out what you may have in common. Don't forget to implement your steps on research and red flags.

Part 4:

Continue working on your goals from Step 9, by networking with people who have similar goals. It's always a pleasant feeling to connect with people who can relate to what you're doing.

Part 5:

This is the most important part of this activity. Find something you like to do all by yourself. Find a nice quiet place and do something that requires just you. Always make time for yourself. Once you find it and the time, write it on your calendar as a daily, weekly, or monthly activity.

			Sunday
			Monday
			Tuesday
			Wednesday
			Thursday
			Friday
			Saturday

Step 16: Take the Extra Step

Sarah:

He passed away in 1989 from throat cancer, he was only 58 years old. He couldn't eat and had a tube com'n out of his stomach. His sister had come help take care of him. I prayed that he would get better, but he never did. I felt like part of me was gone when he died. I dreamt about him every night for years. I had a vision that he came to me as a dove and shitted on me. He said anything that he did to displease me, he was sorry. I will never forget that he was a good dancer and had a beautiful voice. He could also tap dance like nothing I'd ever seen before.

And one thing I can say, is time erases a lot of memories—some good but mostly bad.

Hana:

I thought about suicide because I just wanted to die. But I'm still here, still pushing through.

Jane:

I learned about myself through the years, and I'm still learning. I still want to someday own my own business. Retiring in a nice community is new goals. My three children are all doing well with their families and reaching their goals. Seeing them as three strong women tackling the world is therapeutic and motivates me to keep pushing through.

Nicole:

My grandmother told me her pains come from losing her husband. She retold the stories of them loving each other as often as she could. She always warns me not to let anything stand between me and the person I love. I like to watch my grandma. I listen to her as if I was a child again. She likes to sing an old song—"The Way We Were" by an artist she can never remember. It's comforting somehow.

Jawana:

Mandatory therapy was a part of my probation, but I kept going even after I was no longer required to go. I had nightmares for a long time, as I recalled what happened in my mind. Therapy helped me get my life on track.

MJ:

Five years and two children later, my partner and I are now discussing marriage as a blended family, something I thought I would never heal enough to have. And since my partner knows my journey and has walked some of it with me, he appreciates my growth and how I was able to reach this point in our relationship.

Salina:

My daughter is seventeen years old now, and I fear that she will start looking for love in all the wrong places. She recently experienced her first heartbreak and I could feel her pain. I felt my own pain all over again.

YOU MADE IT!

Never forget how you began this journey and always be proud of where you are. Your last activity will be to teach others. Show them the way. Be their circle of support, guide them during their journey of self-identity, help them to see their self-worth, and protect them from those who want to hurt them. Mentor them. Love them like a sister. Love them like a mother, or a daughter. They are who you were, and they need you. This is how you'll continue to heal. This is how you will continue to live. This is how you will find love.

Now it's time to tell your story.

Dear journal, here's my story:

About the Author:

Known to her followers as "Lady Connect", Melissa Davis started from humble beginnings. Born and raised in Philadelphia's lower class, she quickly discovered her passion for writing; she started creating poems and stories when she was eight years old. By the time she was in high school, Davis knew her writing and outgoing personality would take her far. In 2007, Davis entered a University of Pennsylvania writing competition and won a 1,000 dollar college scholarship.

During her first year at Penn State University, Davis was featured in the school's *Best of Freshman Writing* magazine for her story, "I am Melissa". She went on to win Playwright of the Year, publish articles in *The Berks Collegian*, and place 3rd in a campus-wide poetry contest. Davis would become Lead Editor for *Shadows of Birds,* a campus literary magazine, before graduating in 2015. Shortly after earning her degree, Davis taught the most vulnerable students in Philadelphia's Public School District as a substitute teacher. Seeing that parents transferred their lack of self-love to their children, Davis realized where she needed to focus her teaching. In 2018, Davis decided to teach adults about self-love.

Today, Davis continues to write while building her brand. She's also the founder and President of Millennium Connections, a match-making service that also focuses on education, safe dating, and personal development. Millennium Connections is scheduled to launch its first holistic online curriculum in early 2021.

Follow "Lady Connect":

YouTube: Millennium Connections TV
Facebook: www.facebook.com/ladyconnect
Instagram: @ms.lady.connect

Made in the USA
Monee, IL
09 September 2021